Tiffany and Max Investigate

I Talk You Talk Press

CONTENTS

I Talk You Talk Press

CHAPTER ONE

Tiffany is very small. She is also very pretty. She has blonde hair and big blue eyes. When she was young, her hair was long. Her classmates called her 'Barbie'.

Now she is in her first year at university. Her hair is shorter. No one calls her 'Barbie' anymore, but everyone says she is cute.

Tiffany hates being cute. *I want to be tall,* she thinks. *I want a different face and different hair. I want a different name.*

Tiffany has a boyfriend. His name is Max. She loves him very much. One of the reasons she loves Max is because he doesn't think she is cute. He thinks she is very clever. And Max calls her 'Tiff'.

Max is a university student too. He is studying computer science. He is an A student. He is very tall and thin. He has red-brown hair.

Max has a hobby. He likes collecting insects. Sometimes on Saturdays or Sundays, Max goes to the forest near the university to look for new and interesting insects. He always asks Tiffany to go with him.

Tiffany thinks insects are boring, but she loves Max, so she always says 'yes'.

One Sunday afternoon, Tiffany and Max ride their bicycles to a different part of the forest. It is near the river. They have never been to this part of the forest before.

Max takes his insect box and walks between the trees. It has been raining, but Tiffany finds a nice dry place to sit near the river. It is hot and sunny, and Tiffany is tired. She falls asleep.

A little while later, there is a loud noise, and she wakes up. *What was that noise? Did something fall into the river?* she thinks.

She looks at the river, and after one or two minutes, she sees a person in the water. She runs towards the water. *Someone fell into the river. I have to save them,* she thinks. Then she sees that the person in the river is dead.

Tiffany turns and runs into the forest. "Max! Max! Where are you?" she shouts.

She can't find Max. She falls over. There is blood on her knee, but she gets up and keeps running.

Suddenly, Max is there. He hugs Tiffany.

"Tiff! What's wrong?"

Tiffany is crying. She is shaking. "Max! I saw a body in the river!"

Max holds her tightly. "It's OK. We'll go and look."

Tiffany doesn't want to go back to the river, but she knows they have to go back.

They walk back to the river. There is no body. There is nothing strange. Everything is normal.

Tiffany can't believe it. "I saw a body! It was there!" She points to the water.

"OK, Tiff. Maybe the river carried the body away. We have to call the police."

Max takes out his smartphone. "There is no signal. I can't call the police from here."

He takes Tiffany's hand. "Come on. We must go back to town."

They ride their bicycles to the police station near the university.

"How can I help you?" asks the policeman at the front desk.

"I saw a dead body in the river," says Tiffany.

The policeman puts up his hand. "Stop," he says. He opens a screen on his computer. "What's your name?"

"Tiffany Banks."

"Where do you live?"

"Two three seven A College Avenue."

"And how old are you?"

"Twenty," says Tiffany.

The policeman laughs.

"Twenty?"

Tiffany knows the policeman does not believe her. She is angry. She takes her student ID card from her wallet and gives it to the policeman.

The policeman reads the card. He looks surprised. He gives it back to her.

Then he asks, "Where is the body?"

"In the river," says Tiffany.

"It's a big river. I need more information," says the policeman.

Max takes out his smartphone and opens Google Maps. He finds the place.

He shows the screen to the policeman. "It was here," says Max.

"Did you see the body, Sir?" asks the policeman.

"No," says Max. "Tiff came to find me, but when we got back to the river, the body was gone."

"Oh," says the policeman. "The body was gone."

He looks at Tiffany. "Tell me what happened."

"I was sitting next to the river. It was hot and I fell asleep. A loud noise woke me up. And then I saw the body! I knew the person was dead. I ran to find Max. He came back with me, but the dead body had gone."

"I think you had a bad dream," says the policeman. "I don't think there was any dead body in the river."

"But I saw it! I wasn't dreaming!" Tiffany is shouting.

The policeman stands up. "Please go away. It was a bad dream, or you are making up stories. You are wasting my time. Go away."

Tiffany doesn't want to go, but Max pulls her outside. "We have to go," he says. "Or you will be in big trouble."

Outside the police station, Tiffany starts to cry. She is crying because she is very, very angry.

"That policeman thinks I'm a silly little girl!"

"Listen," says Max. "You are not a silly little girl. You are a very smart young woman."

"Thanks, Max," says Tiffany. "You believe me, don't you? You believe I saw a body in the river."

"Yes, I do." He looks at his phone. "Oh no! It's six pm already! I have a test tomorrow morning. I have to go home and study. I'll meet you in the café at the university tomorrow. I'll be there at twelve thirty pm."

Max jumps on his bicycle and rides away.

CHAPTER TWO

Tiffany doesn't sleep well on Sunday night. She remembers the dead face in the water.

She has no classes on Monday mornings, but she gets out of bed early. She has a plan.

She rides back to the forest. She finds the same place by the river. She looks carefully, but there is nothing.

The river carried the body away, she thinks. *So maybe the river carried the body down the river before I saw it. I'll go and look a little way up the river.*

She walks around the trees and bushes near the river, and soon she finds a narrow, muddy road that goes down to the side of the river.

She can see the marks of tyres in the mud. *Maybe someone drove a car or truck here. Maybe someone brought the body here and threw it in the water,* she thinks.

Tiffany takes out her smartphone. There is no signal, but she can take photographs. She photographs the tyre marks in the mud. She takes a pen from her pocket and puts it down next to the tyre marks. *Later, I can measure the size of the tyres.* She takes more photographs.

She is very busy and interested, but suddenly she has a bad feeling.

I think someone is here. I think someone is watching me! I was OK before, but now I am very scared.

Tiffany runs back to her bicycle and rides out of the forest as fast as she can. When she is out of the forest, she sees a small café. She rides behind the café and hides her bike. She locks it and goes into the café. She sits at a table near the window and orders a coffee.

She watches the road. *Was there someone in the forest? Did they follow me?* she thinks.

After 30 minutes, Tiffany relaxes. No cars come out of the forest. Maybe no one is following her.

She pays for her coffee, and rides back to the university to meet Max.

Max is sitting at their favourite table. He is eating a hamburger and drinking coke. He has ordered a chicken sandwich and a milkshake for Tiffany.

Tiffany sits down and asks, "How was your test? Did you know the answers?"

"It was fine. No problem," says Max.

Tiffany smiles. Max always says the same thing. He is a very good student. He doesn't have any problems with tests.

"You look tired," he says. "Did you sleep well?"

"No, I didn't. Every time I closed my eyes, I saw the face of the dead person. So this morning I went back to the forest."

"What!" Max is shocked. "Why did you go back?"

"The policeman didn't believe me. I was angry. I wanted to look again. Maybe I would remember something."

"The body has gone, Tiff," says Max. "There is nothing to see in the forest."

Tiffany takes out her smartphone. "I walked up the river. I found a place where a car or small truck can drive to the side of the river. I found these tyre marks. Look!"

Max looks at the photographs. He is very interested. But he says, "Maybe they are useful, but maybe not. Are these marks connected to the body? We don't know. Maybe a fisherman drove his car to the side of the river. Did you see anyone in the forest?"

"No," says Tiffany slowly. "But when I was taking these photographs, I suddenly got a bad feeling. I thought 'Someone is watching me'."

Max's face is white. "Oh no! Maybe you were in danger. What did you do?"

"I ran to my bicycle and rode away very quickly. I went to the café on the road near the forest. I watched. No cars came out of the forest."

Max is worried, but he doesn't want Tiffany to be frightened. "OK. I know you saw the dead body, but today you are tired. Maybe you imagined that someone was watching you. You have to tell me more. You saw a 'dead body', but was it a man or a woman? Was it old or young? What did you see?"

Tiffany drinks her milkshake and thinks. "I was sleeping, and a noise woke me up. I looked at the river and soon I saw a face above the water. I could see a body under the water. I think it was a man's face. Not a young person. But I only looked at it for a few seconds, then I ran to find you."

"Was it moving?"

"Uh, oh. I don't know. Maybe yes. Because when I looked at the river after I woke up, there was nothing. And then I saw it."

Students in the café are standing up and walking towards the door. Tiffany looks at the big clock on the wall. "I have to go. I have my French class in ten minutes."

"OK," says Max. "Please send me the photographs you took in the forest this morning. I have an idea."

"Yes. I'll do it as soon as I can." Tiffany hurries out of the café.

Max buys another coke. He has no more classes today, so he opens a game app on his phone and starts to play.

A text message arrives. It's from Tiffany. --- *The teacher is late! Here are the photographs.* ---

Max looks at the photographs. They are too small to see the tyre pattern clearly. He sends them to his laptop. Then he takes his laptop out of his bag and signs in.

He opens the photographs. The images are much bigger and he can see clearly. He sees the pen lying next to the tyre marks. *Clever Tiff,* he thinks. *We can see the pattern, and we know the size.*

He opens Google and types in 'tyre track patterns'. Max is very surprised. He gets more than four million results!

He clicks on the 'Image' icon. There are many pictures of tyres. He tries to match Tiffany's photographs with the images on the screen, but it is difficult. Max is confused. *There is too much information. I don't know anything about tyres,* he thinks. *I need an expert.*

Max remembers a student in one of his classes. His name is Foster. He knows Foster has a part-time job at a company that repairs and sells tyres.

Tomorrow I'll find Foster and ask him to help me.

CHAPTER THREE

The next morning, Max finds Foster in the library. Foster's head is on the table. He is sleeping. Max wakes him up.

"Hi, Foster," he says. "How was the test yesterday?"

Foster looks up from his computer. "Terrible! I'm sure I failed. How about you?"

"I thought it was OK," says Max. "Do you have some free time? I want some help."

Foster is surprised. *Max is the best student in the class. How can I help him?* But he says, "OK."

"We can't talk here. Come to the café with me. I will buy you a cup of coffee."

"Sure," says Foster. "I'm bored. My head hurts. I want to have a rest."

In the café, Max opens his laptop computer and signs in. "I have photographs of some tyre tracks. I want to know the car tyres they are from. Can you help me?" He shows Tiffany's photographs to Foster.

Foster looks at the photographs carefully. He looks at them many times. "Hmm. They are interesting. There are front wheel and back wheel tracks. It's not a car. I think it's a small truck. It's strange. The tyres are from different companies. Two of the tyres are very popular brands. I have seen them many times. But there are two patterns I don't know. Can you send these photographs to me? My boss knows everything about tyres. I only work on Saturdays and Sundays. So I will show him the photographs on Saturday."

"Thank you," says Max.

Foster looks at Max. "But why do you want to know?"

Max doesn't want to tell Foster about Tiffany and the dead body.

"No special reason," he says. "I saw these photographs and I was interested."

Foster doesn't believe Max, but he thinks, *No problem. If I help Max now, maybe he will help me with my study sometime.*

Tiffany and Max have a busy week, so they don't meet again until Friday.

On Friday night, they meet some friends for pizza. Then they go back to Tiffany's apartment. They drink coffee and watch a movie, but the movie is not very good. Tiffany seems sleepy. She rubs her eyes.

"Are you sleeping better now?" asks Max. "Is the face of the dead body still worrying you?"

"I'm sleeping a little better, but I can't stop thinking. Who was the dead person I saw?"

"If someone died, then someone is missing!" Max is excited. "We must look in all the newspapers. Maybe there is a report about a missing person!"

"I don't buy the newspaper," says Tiffany.

"That's OK," says Max. "We can find all the news online. Where's your laptop computer?"

Tiffany brings her laptop to the kitchen table. Max searches for reports of missing people.

"The face looked like an old man?" he asks Tiffany.

"Yes, I think so. It was all so quick!" she says.

"There was a news report this morning. No one has seen a man called Abner Costello since last Friday. He has a small farm outside the city. His neighbours were worried. So yesterday, they called the police. The police say Mr Costello's house was empty, and no one had given food to the animals. They are asking people to look out for him."

"Maybe I saw Mr Costello's body in the water!" Tiffany is excited. "We have to tell the police."

"No, Tiff," says Max. "The policeman didn't believe you. The police will not believe you now. We need more information. Maybe Foster can tell us something."

"Who's Foster?" asks Tiffany.

"He's a guy in my class. He works at a tyre shop. I gave him copies of your photographs. He will show them to his boss tomorrow morning."

Tiffany rubs her eyes again. Max laughs. "I'll go home. You need to sleep. I'll call you after Foster contacts me."

Next morning, Tiffany sleeps late. She feels better. She looks at the news on her laptop. She finds a new item about the missing man, Abner Costello. The headline says --- *Have You Seen This Man?* ---

The item says ---*Mr Costello lived alone. He didn't talk to people. One neighbour said, 'We are worried. There are many stories about Mr Costello. He never goes to the bank. So some people think that he keeps a lot of money in his house.'*---

There is also a photograph.

Tiffany looks at the image for a long time. *Is that the face I saw? Maybe. I'm not sure.*

Her smartphone rings. Max is calling.

"Hi Max," says Tiffany. "Do you have any news?"

"Yes!" says Max. "Foster called me. The tyre tracks you photographed come from a small truck. They are strange, because each tyre is from a different company. The best news is that Foster's boss has fixed those tyres many times. He knows the owner of the truck! The owner is Abner Costello!"

"What!" Tiffany is very surprised. "So maybe Mr Costello drove down to the river. He got out of his truck and fell in the water."

"No. That can't be true," says Max. "We have to talk. Can you meet me for coffee?"

Tiffany showers and dresses quickly. *I forgot to tell Max about the photograph in the news,* she thinks. *I will tell him when we meet. I think it's the same face, but I'm not sure.*

CHAPTER FOUR

Max and Tiffany meet at their favourite downtown café.

They order extra large milk coffees and sit at a small table outside. Max puts his laptop on the table and turns it on.

Tiffany feels a little angry. "Max! I want to talk to you! You don't need your laptop!"

Max laughs, but his face is red. "Sorry, Tiff," he says. "What do you want to tell me?"

She tells him about the photograph in the paper. "They are still looking for Mr Costello," she says. "I looked and looked at the photograph, but I'm not sure. Mr Costello is wearing a hat. His face is not so clear. Could we find another photograph somewhere?"

"Hmm," says Max. "I could hack into the city records and get his ID photograph for his driver's licence."

"Can you do that? That would be great!" Tiffany is smiling.

"I was joking!" says Max.

Tiffany is disappointed. "So you can't do it."

"Well," says Max slowly. "I can do it. It's easy. But I don't want to. It's against the law."

"Oh. So what can we do?" asks Tiffany.

"We know that Mr Costello's truck was next to the river."

"Yes! And maybe he fell into the water!" says Tiffany.

"No. That can't be true. You saw the dead face a short time after the noise woke you up. Someone who falls into the river shouts. They try to swim. You didn't see or hear anything. And tell me. If it was Mr Costello in the water, who drove the truck away?"

"Oh," says Tiffany. "So it wasn't him. He drove his truck down to the river some other time and drove away."

"Maybe," says Max. "But maybe, not. Can I use my laptop now?"

"Yes!" laughs Tiffany.

Max turns the laptop around so that Tiffany can see the screen.

"The tyre marks you found were in the mud. Here are the weather records. It was hot and dry every day for a week before we went to the forest. Then it rained a lot on Saturday night. The rain made the ground wet. It was muddy. So the tyre marks show that Abner Costello's truck was next to the river sometime on Sunday."

Tiffany is thinking hard. "Abner Costello drove his truck to the river in the morning. The body wasn't Mr Costello. We were there in the afternoon."

"But Tiff," says Max. "Maybe the body was Mr Costello. No one has seen him for a week. I have an idea. Someone killed Mr Costello. The killer put his body in the truck. On Sunday afternoon, the killer drove the truck to the river and threw the body in the river."

"We have to tell the police," says Tiffany.

"The police won't listen to us. It's only my idea," says Max. "And we didn't see or hear a truck."

Max is playing football in the afternoon and Tiffany is going shopping with friends, so they leave the café.

"Keep thinking, Max!" says Tiffany.

"You too," laughs Max.

After football, Max goes to a bar with his team. His friends are drinking beer and talking about the game. Max is very quiet. He doesn't feel like drinking beer. He is thinking hard about the mystery.

His smartphone rings. He looks at the screen. Foster is calling him. It is too noisy in the bar, so he goes outside. "Hi Foster," he says.

Foster is excited. "I think I found the truck! Abner Costello's truck! Do you know he is missing? The police are looking for him."

"Talk slower, Foster," says Max. "Where did you find the truck?"

"We put new tyres on a Mercedes today. It belongs to a rich guy in the next town. He is a good customer. My boss told me to deliver it to this rich guy and come back on the bus. "It was wonderful driving that Mercedes! I want to buy one!"

"Foster," says Max. "The truck. Where did you see the truck?"

"I was on the bus, and I was looking out the window," says Foster. "I saw the back of a small truck. It was in some bushes."

"How do you know it's Mr Costello's truck?" asks Max.

"My boss told me it was an old Dodge truck, and it was red. I saw the back of a red Dodge truck. But I can't be sure until I look at the tyres," says Foster. "Shall we tell the police?"

"Not yet," says Max. "We have to be sure. I'll borrow my brother's car. I'll pick you up and we can go together."

"It's OK. I'll meet you there. I'll go on my motorbike."

Foster tells Max the place where he saw the truck.

"OK," says Max. "I'll send you a text message when I leave town. Thanks Foster."

Max calls his brother Owen. "Can I borrow your car tonight?" he asks.

"It's Saturday night. Are you crazy?" says Owen, laughing.

"Please, Owen. It's important."

"OK. I'll call my girlfriend and tell her we will drive her car tonight. Where are you?"

"I'm at the Pathways Bar."

"What! You can't drive my car if you have been drinking!"

"I only drank Coke. I'm safe to drive," says Max.

"OK, I'll be there in about forty minutes."

I have to tell Tiff, thinks Max. He calls Tiffany and tells her his plan.

"I'm coming too," she says. "I'll come to Pathways Bar and wait with you."

Max looks at the sky. It's getting dark.

"Bring a torch," he says.

CHAPTER FIVE

Max sees Foster. He is standing next to his motorbike at the side of the road. Max finds a place to park the car. He walks towards Foster.

Foster sees a very small person getting out of the car. "Are your parents out tonight?" he asks.

"No," says Max. "Why?"

"Your little sister has come with you."

"That's Tiff. She's my girlfriend."

"Wow! She's cute!"

"Don't let Tiff hear you call her cute. It makes her very angry."

Tiffany is carrying a big torch. "Hi," she says. "You must be Foster. I'm Tiffany, but please call me Tiff." She gives the torch to Foster.

Foster takes the torch, but he doesn't move. "I know Abner Costello is missing. But why are you so interested? Where did the photographs come from? You have to tell me."

Tiffany and Max tell Foster about the body in the river. They tell him that the policeman didn't believe Tiffany.

"So I went back to the river and looked," says Tiffany. "I found the marks from tyres. I took photographs. I was scared because I thought 'someone is watching me'.

"I always wanted to be a detective!" Foster is excited. "Let's go and look at the truck!"

They follow Foster into the bushes, but suddenly, Foster stops.

"The truck is gone!" he shouts. "It was here. I saw it! But now it's gone."

He shines the torch over the ground. "But there is some mud here. I can see tyre marks."

He kneels on the ground. He looks carefully. "It was Abner Costello's truck. The marks are the same. Where is the truck now? Who drove it away?"

Tiffany takes her smartphone from her pocket. Foster shines the torch on the tracks, and she takes more photographs. They go back to the car and talk.

"No one has seen Mr Costello for more than a week," says Max. "But maybe he is driving his truck around."

"Or maybe it is someone else," says Tiffany. "We have to tell the police!"

"I don't know," says Max slowly. "Maybe Foster's boss will help us."

"Yes!" says Foster. "We will show him the photographs. We will tell him everything. He will say 'these tracks came from Abner Costello's truck'. The police will believe him. I'll call him."

Foster calls his boss, but there is no answer from his boss's smartphone. He calls the home number, but no one picks up the phone.

"Maybe my boss didn't charge his phone. And maybe he is out tonight," says Foster. "I will see him tomorrow. I can ask him then."

"Yes, please," says Max. "We can't do anything more tonight. Let's go home."

"OK," says Foster. "But I need the photographs Tiffany took tonight."

Tiffany sends the new photographs to Foster's phone, and they leave.

Max drives Tiffany to her apartment. "Tomorrow we can talk to the police," he says.

Back in her apartment, Tiffany feels tired and hungry. She makes a sandwich and drinks a glass of milk.

It's only 10:00pm, but I will go to bed now, she thinks. *Tomorrow, Foster's boss, Max and Foster will go to the police. The police will believe my story. I don't have to worry anymore.*

CHAPTER SIX

Tiffany's smartphone rings. It wakes her up.

She looks at the caller ID. It's Max. She looks at the time. It's midnight.

"Oh no, Max!" she shouts into the phone. "You woke me up!"

Max doesn't listen. He is very excited. "Look at the local news on your laptop," he says. "It's very interesting."

Tiffany goes into her kitchen. Her laptop is on the table. She turns it on and finds the local news. She puts her smartphone on speaker mode.

"OK, Max," she says. "What is interesting?"

"They found the body of a man on the beach, where the river goes into the sea," he says.

Tiffany is still very sleepy. "What river?" she asks.

"Tiff!" shouts Max. "Our river! The river next to the forest. The river where you saw the body!"

"Oh!" Tiffany looks at the news items and finds the right one. She opens it.

Max is talking. "Quiet Max!" says Tiffany. "I'm reading."

The item says --- *The body was in the water for a long time. The police think it is Mr Costello. His head was damaged. Someone found Mr Costello's truck in the river. The police think it was an accident.* ---

Suddenly Tiffany hears a noise. She looks up. There is a strange man in her kitchen! He walks to the table.

"Who are you?" she shouts.

The man is big. He is dirty. "You don't know me," he says. "But I know you. You are Tiffany Banks. You go to the university."

Tiffany is very scared, but she says, "How do you know?"

"I was hiding in the forest on Monday morning. I saw you in the forest. You were taking photographs next to the river. You were taking photographs of the ground where I parked the old man's truck. I thought 'she will talk to the police'. So I have been looking for you."

"But how did you find me? How do you know my name?" asks Tiffany.

The strange man smiles. It is not a nice smile. "I saw your bicycle. It has a university sticker on it. I waited around the university every day until I saw you. I remembered you well because you are so small and cute. Then I followed you. It was easy. Your name is on the letter box for this apartment."

Max is still on the phone. He can hear everything! He panics. *Tiff is in danger! I have to call the police, but I have to listen to this man.*

Max runs out of his apartment. He has no shoes on. He leaves the door open. He runs down the road towards Tiffany's apartment.

He sees a taxi. He jumps in and says, "Call the police! Tell them to go to two three seven A College Avenue. It's an emergency! There is a man in the apartment. I think he is a killer!"

The taxi driver stares at Max, but he calls the police. Max is still listening on his smartphone.

He hears Tiffany say, "But the police think it was an accident. They found Mr Costello's body on a beach. Someone saw his truck in the water. You are safe."

"Maybe you know it wasn't an accident. Maybe you know I killed the old man. I'll only be safe when you are dead."

"Quickly," shouts Max. "Drive to two three seven A College Avenue! The police might be too late! We must save Tiff!"

I have to keep him talking, thinks Tiffany.

"Why did you kill Mr Costello?" she asks.

"I heard he had a lot of money in his house. I went there. I asked 'where is the money?' He wouldn't tell me.

"I punched him. I hit him very hard. He fell and hit his head. He died. So I put his body in his truck. The next afternoon I drove to the river and threw his body into the water. I put the truck in some bushes by the side of the road. But the police were looking for the old man and his truck. So early Saturday night, I drove it into the river."

The man takes out a knife. "I don't think anyone saw me come here, but I'm not sure."

He jumps towards Tiffany. "No!" shouts Tiffany.

Max hears loud noises. Tiffany is shouting. "Help!"

There is a bang. Then there is no sound from his phone.

The taxi stops outside the apartment building. Max and the taxi driver can hear police cars, but they are far away.

They run up the stairs. Max is very worried. The door to Tiffany's apartment is open.

In the kitchen, they find Tiffany sitting at the table. She is wearing her pyjamas. There are tears on her face, and there is blood on her arm.

She is holding her smartphone. "My phone is broken," she says.

Max runs to Tiffany and hugs her. "Oh Tiff," he says. "I thought 'you will die'."

The taxi driver is looking at the floor. "Look at this," he says. "How did she do it?"

Max looks. There is a large man lying on the floor. He is not moving. Next to his head is a big, heavy pot.

"I think I was lucky," says Tiffany. "He ran at me with his knife. He cut my arm. I ran behind the table. I threw a chair at him. It didn't hurt him, but he fell over. I picked up my biggest pot and hit his head. Then he didn't move. Is he dead?"

The taxi driver puts his fingers on the man's neck. "No. He's not dead."

Then they hear the police running up the stairs.

Max smiles at Tiffany. "I think the police will believe you now," he says.

CHAPTER SEVEN

The police take the man away. "He will go to the hospital," says a policeman. "But he will be OK."

A police doctor puts a bandage on Tiffany's arm. The police ask many questions. Max tells them about the body in the river. He tells them about Tiffany's photographs. He tells them about Foster and Foster's boss.

The taxi driver tells the police about Max and the drive to Tiffany's apartment. The police tell the taxi driver he can go home.

It is 3:00am. Max and Tiffany are very tired.

"So many questions!" says Max to the police.

"Two more questions," says the chief policeman. He looks at Max. "How did you know what was happening here?"

"Tiff was reading the news on her laptop. She put her phone on speaker mode. I could hear everything."

"I understand," says the policeman. "Second question. How did such a small, cute girl beat this very bad man?"

Max holds Tiffany's hand. "She's not a small, cute girl. She is a very smart, strong woman."

THANK YOU

Thank you for reading Tiffany and Max Investigate (Word count: 5,497) We hope you enjoyed it.

If you would like to read more graded readers, please visit our website http://www.italkyoutalk.com

Other Level 2 graded readers include
Adventure in Rome
Andre's Dream
A Passion for Music
Christmas Tales
Danger in Seattle
Don't Come Back
Dressed for Success
Elspeth and the Visitor
Finders Keepers…
How Did You Meet?
Hunted in Hong Kong
John Sees a Murder
Marcy's Bakery
Men's Konkatsu Tales
Message in a Bottle
Murder in Marrakech
Murder on Whale Island

Neighbours
Salaryman Secrets!
Stories for Halloween
The Cruise Ship
The Perfect Wedding
The House in the Forest
The Kindness of Strangers
The School on Bolt Street
Train Travel
Trouble in Paris
Who's There?
Women's Konkatsu Tales

ABOUT THE AUTHOR

I Talk You Talk Press is an award-winning Japan-based publisher of language textbooks, graded readers and language learning/teaching resources. We won the Language Learner Literature Award in 2019 and 2020.

Our team is made up of highly experienced language teachers and translators, who have all studied at least one additional language to an advanced level.

This experience enables us to design our materials from the perspective of both the teacher and the learner. We consult with both teachers and language learners when designing our textbooks and graded readers, and test our materials extensively in the classroom before publication.

We are a fast-growing press, and currently publish graded readers for learners of English. We publish new graded readers monthly.

9 7 8 4 9 1 0 9 7 1 0 1 8